HISTORY
FOR
PEACE
TRACTS

How do we understand what was, grapple with
what is and prepare for what is likely to be,
as a nation, as a people, as a community,
as individuals?

This series is an attempt to address this question
by putting into print thoughts, ideas and
concerns of some of South Asia's most
seminal thinkers.

In memory of Kozo Yamamura (1934–2017)

HISTORY FOR PEACE TRACTS

KRISHNA KUMAR
Learning to Live with the Past

YOUSUF SAEED
Partitioning Bazaar Art

RAJEEV BHARGAVA
Reimagining Indian Secularism

DEEPA SREENIVAS
Remaking the Citizen for New Times

The Idea of India

A Dialogue

GAYATRI CHAKRAVORTY SPIVAK

ROMILA THAPAR

LONDON NEW YORK CALCUTTA

The text in this volume is a revised transcript of a conversation held at the 2017 History for Peace conference, *The Idea of India*.

Seagull Books, 2024

© Gayatri Chakravorty Spivak
and Romila Thapar, 2024

First published in volume form
by Seagull Books, 2024

ISBN 978 1 80309 384 0

British Library Cataloguing-in-Publication Data

A catalogue record for this book
is available from the British Library

Typeset by Seagull Books, Calcutta, India

Printed and bound by WordsWorth India,
New Delhi, India

Ideas have a way of wandering about—
you can't pinpoint their origins.

GAYATRI CHAKRAVORTY SPIVAK. Although we are both guests on the stage, I feel as though I'm welcoming my old friend to Kolkata, because this is the first time that I've seen her here. Presidency University, of course, has had the good sense to give her an honorary doctorate.

This is a conversation that began long ago, many, many years ago, sometimes between the two of us, sometimes in front of an audience, sometimes in New York where I acknowledged the incredible role that the humanities imagination plays in many of the things that she has done. But today I'm only the questioner—because it's about teaching history, and god knows I don't know anything about teaching history. So what I really want to ask Romila is, how does one teach the idea of India?

ROMILA THAPAR. Let me begin by thanking Seagull for this unique opportunity. Gayatri and I have often chatted in the privacy of, should I say, our homes, in New York, in Delhi. We've had long conversations, teased each other, joked with each other. This is the first time, as far as I remember, that we're speaking before an audience. So, if we start laughing unstoppably or shouting at each other, you must forgive us. This is just out of sheer friendship.

You've asked a very tough question to start with. What do we mean by the idea of India? Being a historian, I would turn it around a little bit and ask: When did the idea of India come into existence? One can't date it, of course, because one can seldom date ideas with precision. Ideas have a way of wandering about—you can't pinpoint their origins. The idea of India, I think, is a modern idea, a concept which emerges in colonial times. We often hear people saying: Oh yes, the idea of India existed in the Vedic period, it existed in the Gupta period, it existed in the Mughal period, and so on. I would beg to differ with that. We don't really know how people saw themselves in the context of states, nations and countries. We don't even know what names each took. We know, for example, that the Sumerians—now I'm going really back, far back—of the third millennium BCE referred to countries to their east, one in particular with whom they had trade relations, and the items they traded were items that came from the Indus plain. So we assume it's a reference to the Indus civilization, which they seem to have called Meluhha, which we think might be a Sumerian version of the Prakrit *Melukhkha / Milakkha / Milakkhu.*

But in the Vedic period we begin to get textual evidence, references to something called Aryavarta. Now *Aryavarta* is a very interesting term because the place it refers to keeps shifting. In the Vedic texts, it extends from the Doab to just about the middle of the Ganges valley. In the Buddhist texts, the location moves a little eastwards. In the Jaina texts, it moves still further east. By the time you get to Manu and his *Manava-Dharmashastra*, he's talking about Aryavarta being the land between the Himalayas and the Vindhyas, and north of the land between the two seas. That is not quite the India that we speak of today. Similarly with Jambudvipa, which Ashoka refers to it in his inscriptions. We do not know where it was nor what its boundaries were. Bharatvarsha is also vague and changeable. Al-Hind, which comes into use from about the twelfth century CE onwards, refers to all the land across the Indus when looked at from West Asia. Then come the British, and they start referring to this part of the country as India, from the Greek *Indós,* referring to the Indus. (The Vedic texts also mention the Sapta-Sindhu, referred to by the ancient Iranians as the Hapta-Hendu, the *s* and the *h* being interchangeable.)

Now, what did the British mean? They talk about India when they've conquered certain parts of Eastern India, and have gone on to conquer other parts of the peninsula and then moved north. With each conquest, the boundaries change until, finally at the end of the nineteenth century, the entire subcontinent is painted red—that is the India of the British Empire.

Is this when the concept of India, the idea of India, comes into being? Possibly, but it's a territorial concept. The idea of India is, of course, much more than territory—it's culture, language, religion . . . all that is assumed. When does *that* begin? My guess is—although I'm not a historian of modern India, and I may be completely wrong here—that one of the most interesting decades of our times were the 1920s. What happened in the 1920s? You had, first of all, the Indian National Congress, with Gandhi trying to convert the movement into a mass movement, which he successfully did. I'm not going to quibble with the subaltern-studies perspective and others on how far it truly was as a mass movement but, technically, yes, it certainly included a very large number of people, and the idea of India began to take hold because the end, the purpose of it, was the independence of the nation that was being created.

But the 1920s also saw the development of two other notions linked to the idea of India. There was the Muslim League that asked for Pakistan, which was a negation of the idea of India since it is a truncated version of British India. Countering this was the establishment of the Hindu Mahasabha, in the 1920s again, which gives way to the RSS wherein the idea of India is very clearly enunciated as the Hindu Rashtra.

Now you've already got three ideas—not one but three. The Communist Party of India, founded in the 1920s, retained the untruncated India but defined it as a socialist state. So I think the 1920s is really where the discussion should start in terms of not a single idea but the opening out of possible ways of looking at these ideas—why they happened, and what the consequences were. We know about the creation of the two nations, and then, later, Pakistan splitting into two with the emergence of Bangladesh. Associated with these was the notion of Independence, and what was being sought at the time of Independence. What was this idea of India as conceived by the anticolonial national movement, the biggest movement at that time? How were those people visualizing the idea of India, how were they thinking of where Independence begins?

SPIVAK. Well that's a big one. Now I'm going to respond a little to what you said, which was the question I asked you in your house in November. First of all, of course, I am deeply suspicious of ideas. We cannot proceed without ideas—they're a convenience—but they're also very dangerous, they're like a lid you put on a boiling pot under which they begin to—your word is crystallize, right?—take control of an entire seething, boiling mass of all kinds of thoughts. Having spent a life trying to learn from the literary, I'm a little afraid of ideas.

I also feel, in some ways—and again, I'm really only speaking as an Indian—that 'I'm not an Indian'. It's true, you can scream at me, you have screamed at me, remember when you said, 'Why are you teaching South Asia at all, you produce these students who don't know anything?' And I stopped. There're very few people in the world from whom I would take that kind of suggestion.

Another thing you told me, when I said, after Edward [Said]'s death, that I would do a biography, was: 'Don't try to research everything historically. If you think something is true and correct because of the way you've lived, put it down,' and so it's the second suggestion that I'm taking up now. It seems to me that there was in the sense of India that we got—I was born in 1942, I was a precocious child, so I remember quite a bit of stuff. Of course, mostly famine, riots and so on. But what we got later— thinking about it, I felt more and more, with my friend Edward Said, that it was a kind of an orientalist discovery of India, a discovery which allowed what Vladimir Ilyich would call the progressive bourgeoisie to think about India in this way, however much they wanted to bring in the masses. Which is why it slowly began to fade away. This is just an Indian person's opinion, an Indian person who knows nothing about India from book learning. This is *my* sense of things. And this is why I wanted to ask you the question, and I wrote it down, the question about what you said to me in a conversation in your house last November: 'When we were active in the Independence struggle as young people, we did not expect the grave problems that would arise as the post-Independence years progressed,' or something to that effect. I'm interested in hearing from you a more detailed explanation of this, including whatever you want to say about the first Independence and the specific hopes that seem not to have fulfilled themselves.

I'm thinking now about the Bangladesh War, of which of course I have a good deal of experience. Both my dear friends, Zafrullah Chowdhury and Sandhya Ray, who was very involved—she gave up her education, at 15 she joined Zafrullah—said: 'We thought that when Independence came in—I could go back to school . . . We didn't realize that that would mean nothing.' And finally, behind it all is Frederick Douglass at Emancipation, saying, 'Now the problems begin.' You have obviously been troubled by this. I really wanted you to say something more about it—I think it's crucial to hear from you what it was that moved you to say it on your own.

THAPAR. I agree with you. I'm also often
suspicious of ideas. Largely because
ideas have a habit of slipping around
and changing their meaning, which is
disturbing. You think they mean
something and you locate them in a
place, and then you discover that they
mean something quite different, and so
on. They're a tricky business. But yes,
the idea. I wonder if I could start with
an anecdote from my school days. Just
to give you a flavour of what it was that
we were doing in our teenage years in
the early 1940s. I was at school in Pune.
My father was in the army and hence
frequently transferred, and we went
from Peshawar to Rawalpindi to Pune.
We arrived in Pune in 1942, at a time
when Gandhiji was in and out of jail.
We were part of the cantonment

culture, one that I wish some cultural historian would work on because it was quite distinctive and a reflection of colonialism. It was different from the entirely Indian city, it was Indians and Brits working together but not really socializing. This was something that struck me even then, about the people who dropped in—and dropping in was a great thing in the evenings. You had nothing better to do, and so you dropped in on friends and sat around. It was always Indians who dropped in, very concerned about what was going on, because this was the 40s. We, as school-going teenagers, would hang around the grown-ups, and often my father would say to me, 'You've listened to everything we've been discussing but don't go about repeating it in school.

Obviously, what we're discussing is meant only for us Indians.' So that consciousness was very strong.

But to return to what happened to me in school. Come 1947, my final year in convent school. A convent school because all of us 'army brats' had recourse to only those schools that had any kind of uniform teaching, and that were geared towards what was then called the Senior Cambridge Exam. About a month before 15 August, Sister Superior sent for me. I went to her, fearful and trembling, thinking, 'What have I done now?' And she said, 'Independence Day is coming on the 15th of August. You're one of the prefects, and we thought that it would be nice if the prefects lowered the Union Jack, raised the Indian flag, planted a sapling, and you would then give a 15-minute speech about what Independence means to you.' I was absolutely aghast, and said, 'You mean me?' and she said, 'Yes, I mean you. Now don't disappoint us, think about it—but do it.'

I came out of her room, and then for nights on end I couldn't sleep. I kept thinking, 'What am I going to say? Fifteen minutes—what am I going to say?' I remember going to my favourite teacher, who happened to be the history and literature teacher, and saying, 'What shall I talk about?' and she said, 'You keep talking about the future with your friends—what do you say? What do you think about the coming of Independence? Just stand up and talk about that.' So what was it that we talked about? We talked about: 'We're now going to find an Indian identity.' Very important to us in those days. What do we mean when we say 'We're Indians'? We're Indians in the context of British colonialism, yes, but now we're going to be Indians without British colonialism—what does that mean?

The second thing we all talked about was: Once colonialism goes, the rules of 'You can't go here, you can't go there,' and 'You can't do this and you can't do that,' all that will go. So what kind of society will we have?

That is what has stayed with me through the years. It's still with me, especially these days. I'm still trying to find out what we mean by an Indian identity, and, my goodness, these days one is thinking very hard about what kind of society we should have. We've been through a socialist pattern and discarded it, we have been trying to establish a democracy, but it seems to get side-tracked what with the Emergency in 1975, and once again we are pursuing activities that can hardly be called democratic. Looking back on the last few decades, the premiership of Nehru was about the only time when we could claim that we were moving towards a democracy.

And after Independence, in the 50s, it was about this and much more that we continued to talk . . . 'We must define our society.' There was a fair bit of socialistic thinking going around in those days, partly inspired by some of Nehru's speeches, partly inspired by other people who said one couldn't have a society without inequality. So we started thinking in terms of a society that would be reasonably equal. Now this inevitably led, in the 60s at least, to an absolute obsession with the economy. Economic growth was the subject of the hour, right through that decade, questions about economic planning, state industrialization, employment, rural development and so on. Any student who had an iota of intelligence wanted to be an economist because that was the subject that mattered. Historians and philosophers were at the bottom of the pile—ancient historians in particular—nobody was interested in all that. And not just economics but also economic growth, statistics, demography, all that went into calculating how to build a society that one could be proud of.

I remember even earlier, in the 50s, for example, before the debates of the 60s in Delhi. I was a student in England, we used give talks all over the place, at meetings of the Workers' Educational Association. Talking about what? About the great new society that was emerging in India. And why did we come back to India? Because it was going to give us the great opportunity to build a new society, a new society to which we would belong and with great pride. There was a kind of innocent belief that Independence was going to bring about all these changes. It was an innocent belief because I guess we hadn't really worked out all the problems. The focus on the economy, on economic change, was so strong that there was much less attention paid to aspects of caste and religion. And so when caste and religion surfaced, we were almost taken by surprise. Where did *those* come from?

And, of course, the other great claim was, 'When freedom comes, we will be free to speak as and how we wish. We will be free to speak the way we want to.' The first shock I had on this issue was when I encountered censorship after Independence. My brother Romesh Thapar was bringing out a fortnightly called *Crossroads* in Bombay. Very left, very revolutionary and socialist. I would go down to Bombay during my holidays and help with the proofreading. On one occasion, a headline stated that the chief minister's action was unacceptable and described it as 'criminal'. And of course, the very next week, the censor hit, and my brother was informed that *Crossroads* had been banned. This demonstrated that freedom doesn't bring freedom of speech, and that you have to be somewhat careful about how you negotiate freedom of speech. The case went to court, and my brother won. It is now quoted invariably as the precedent on matters relating to freedom of speech and it remains a foundational case. Whenever freedom of speech comes up, they all refer to *Romesh Thappar vs The State of Madras*.

We'd all studied the French Revolution, we'd all studied the books that went with it, we'd studied the Russian Revolution . . . so we had these ideas about how India was going to be an ideal society. But it didn't work out that way. And slowly, one began to recognize why not, and what the problems were.

SPIVAK. Of course, what I want you to talk about is precisely what the problems were. But I want to put in my two bits too. My sense of building an Indian society, etc., came about a little bit later . . . Delhi and Calcutta—they're very, very different. My uncle was Jnan Majumdar, so I was in the middle of a kind of intellectual left which was very Calcutta at that time. At any rate, I left the country because Tarak Nath Sen told me I wouldn't get a first class in my MA. My father was dead. I was supporting myself, so I had to kind of buzz off. That's why I left, right?

At that time, we were really at the bottom of the pile, Romila—even below the historians were the literary people. I think I would've been even worse off had I been reading Bengali. Before leaving, our sense was like Dev Anand's in that film, *Guide*, that 'English is only one of the languages of the world, so that when we speak it . . .' Absurd, but that's how it was. 'When we speak Bengali, we will speak wonderful Bengali, and when we speak English we will speak wonderful English,' you know? The first adolescent generation, postcolonial, etc.

So, by the time I left the country, there was an idea of India which did not resemble at all the marching in the streets, and so on. Allen Ginsberg, all that stuff . . . I sang on the harmonium with him, and it was a crazy thing, confronting that India, with ganja and the whatchamacallit and Vajrayana Buddhism and Gary Snyder and Zen . . . All that resembled nothing.

On the other hand, when in 1962, Malcolm X came to Cornell to speak—he started speaking (he was a very mild-mannered man), I remember it so clearly—and the idea of India in my head made me think, 'Gee, this is like Calcutta.' Malcolm X is speaking, I'm 20 years old, sitting in the audience—and that's what I thought. Otherwise, all around me was this other India made up in that way.

Now the diasporics are becoming really important. When you first invited me to teach in India in 1987—remember, I was not invited by the literature section, because I was not French and yet I was doing French theory. So Professor Thapar invited this non-historian (*points to herself*) to teach in the history department—and that is something that should be known, that there's been solidarity between us for a very long time. However, back to '87, and what I began to feel was more and more the difference: I gave a long talk in Bengali, here in Baguiati, on the difference between onabashi and probashi, the expats and the NRIs. *Onabashi* is a made-up word. At that point in time, it had already become important for us not to acknowledge the diasporic image of India, a minority in the United States. Sometimes even a white-identified, good, affirmative-action minority.

Sometimes a minority in that little island off the coast of France. On the other hand, not claiming the kind of 86 per cent majority that was already showing signs of violence. So, at that point, what happened to me was that I turned more and more to thinking about the rural Indian landless illiterate people whose children I taught, who don't even know the word Dalit and yet called themselves SC/STs, and to seeing if there was an idea of India in the largest sector of the electorate. I'm not going to go on about it, because I think we want to hear more about your idea of the problems and so on. But I just wanted to get this said.

Because now it is, in fact, on the rise, this business. Because of what's going wrong abroad, with the new

Khilafat which has a history which is
not known by anybody. It is known, but
it's not known by the young radicals.
And what's happening in France and
the rest of Europe—the rise of the right-
wing. And let's not even talk about the
United States. Of course there is a
certain kind of unity coming in among
the radical diasporics, but it's an
unexamined unity. So that, to an extent,
the continents of Africa and Asia are
becoming adjunct to these radical
diasporics. Which is why we, who do
not want to discourage this, feel that we
have an obligation to talk about those
old nation-state type ideas, of the
'national enterprise', as my friend
Bernard Harcourt calls it.

So how do we re-negotiate the idea
of India as a safe idea? The present

prime minister was just in the United States. Luckily, I wasn't. There we have a certain kind of solidarity emerging which is extremely frightening. Therefore, I just wanted to get that in, in terms of the problems from outside, which is not only *not* disappearing but also increasing. And now, I want to hear a bit more about what you think of as a list of problems.

THAPAR. One of the problems you've touched upon in the notion of the idea of India, or the idea of any place for that matter, is of course that the idea changes—it's not the same all the time. The idea of India that I had in 1947 has changed. Reality begins to impinge on the idea, and the idea takes on a different kind of shape. In the 50s and 60s, the diaspora was seen as something relatively marginal to begin with, it was seen as disgruntled people who are not very happy over here, who are pushing off there because they're getting better jobs and leading a better life. Initially, of course—and I know the UK better than the US—it was a different group of people who went. It was the sailors, and some members of the working class who were especially taken to do specific jobs. Their presence was absolutely marginal. But when it began to change, when professionals started going and the middle-class migrated, then two things happened, as happens even now. One: they did so well that they became, as it were, the role models for the middle class here, and their attitudes therefore became extremely influential. Interestingly, also, they developed a culture which was divorced from the culture of the host country. The culture of the diaspora is a very specific culture—it doesn't really feed into or draw on the culture of the host country, but remains separated, initially at least. My guess is that as long as there isn't a critical mass of Indians in American politics or British politics, or there isn't a lot of intermarriage, it will remain a distinctive community. I may be wrong about this. So, what happens in the diaspora is not something that is to be dismissed. And much of what one might call cultural or religious attitudes of the diaspora tend to have a very direct influence on the middle class here. And, of course, we know that the middle class today has completely different ideas and ideals than it had in the 60s.

I'm always very intrigued by the fact that, on occasion when I switch on the television to watch the news, there are advertisements for private universities. Very often, they show lavish laboratories, foreign scholars coming to lecture. Describing the university, they announce loudly, 'Your destination: Success.' I always ask myself: Surely, the destination of a university is learning, knowledge, thinking. How does it become success? And what is meant by success? Is it making money and having power? And I think that is a very distinctive difference that has crept in.

But I'm going off a little bit. We were talking about what was it that caused a lot of change. I mentioned how there was a tremendous obsession with economic growth and economic change—very legitimate, but it tended not to give enough attention to religion and language and to what is generally described as cultural articulation. There was a tendency to assume that religion is not very important in India, that the political message is much more important. That if we can solve the economic problems, we can solve all the others. Language became a problem, and it was finally solved in the way in which democracy solves all its problems—that is, the numbers in support of linguistic states were counted, and the majority opinion accepted. What linguistic states have done is another issue, is another question, and I think one that impinges very much on the notion of nationalism in the country.

Then, of course, there's the cultural idiom which always tends to be associated in India with the coming in of religion, whether it really is or not. And by this I mean that when people define Indian culture, and this relates a little bit to what you were saying, the idea is not to ask, 'What is the culture of the entire Indian society? What is the culture from top to bottom?' It's always only the culture at the top—that becomes the identity, that becomes the Indian identity. And, in fact, many of the problems we're facing today are precisely because that identity is not sufficiently broad. The identity has not been discussed and debated sufficiently in order to arrive at a point where one can say that, 'Yes, this is perhaps not the ideal identity, but it does approximate the ideas that most people have of what they mean when they say "I am an Indian".'

As a historian, I see this as a heritage of the colonial view of India and Indian culture: the two-nation theory underlined the perspectives on culture and theory as devolving from the Hindu and Muslim communities in a strictly religious sense. Looking beyond the elite was thought to be unnecessary.

SPIVAK. It seems to me also that the idea of India is quite often metonymic of one's language group. The Indians who speak about India abroad quite often have no clue about the fact that it is an extremely multi-everything place. Forget about class and caste—just in terms of cultural differentiation . . . And I think that's a major problem.

I don't even know whether one should think 'India'—that's another question. But if one does, then one should think about Indians who do not resemble one at all. Now that's one of the things that's disappearing today— it's disappearing abroad, it's disappearing at home, and I think it's a tremendous shame. When we were growing up, for example, if something got lost, I'd say, 'Oof-oh! Hajir Pir ke ektu noon jol dite hobe.' You have to give some salt water to Hajir Pir if you want to find. Now it's all Ganesh. If you find something, it's all thanks to Ganesh. I mean, we didn't even think that by giving that salt water to Hajir Pir, we were being middle-class syncretic secularists. It was just a natural thing to do, but those kinds of things have disappeared, you know.

Sometimes, when I see someone abroad and say 'Salaam-Alaikum,' they say, 'Oh, you're Muslim?' I say, 'No, that's also an Indian greeting—what's your problem?' (*Audience laughs*) This is the kind of thing that should be practised in our everyday lives. I think this very, very strongly. So that somehow we begin to think not only of our own identity as *the* Indian identity.

You said that one of the things you were thinking about when Independence came was, 'We talked of economic growth that would end poverty.' Garibi Hatao.

Now here I can say something, because I'm supposed to be an expert on economic growth and social inclusion for the World Economic Forum. I have this wonderful colleague called Xavier Sala-i-Martin who has invented the competitive index. And he says, 'Look, I can tell, because I go to meetings of the World Economic Forum, that when the Ministry of Finance of Rwanda and the Ministry of Finance of Canada come and talk to me, because I show where there are new areas of economic growth, they are not talking about the same thing. But I can talk to both of them. But social inclusion? That's in your hands.' This separation has now gone, totally gone. I'm coming from Ghana. Ghana has just launched its first satellite. There's the diasporic convention, and I'm listening to them. And what are they saying? They're saying, 'Now, we are no longer looking for freedom, we are looking for economic growth.' And this is how the Indians talk about China. So this whole issue of economic growth—of not including social inclusion, of exacerbating the difference between the rich and the poor . . .

Thomas Piketty is a very nice guy but his wonderful Eurocentric book does not take into account how bad things were in the Scandinavian countries in the 90s. Because the Somalis and the Rwandans and the Turks were coming in, the Scandinavians were changing the rules. So they were no longer Piketty's ideal, but he never once writes a sentence about the change. He's also talking about inheritance rather than capital, etc. Just paying taxes and so on is not going to do it. But this particular question has become so identified with the idea of India, this question of economic growth. The middle class is going up, there's electricity all over the place, there are latrines and so on. Economic growth and social inclusion—I think that problem has to be questioned in a completely different way. It perhaps needs the revamping of education from bottom to top, because education is not just learning and knowledge, it is also questions, it is also questioning. I mean, the good education that you were talking about—that is also questioning. That has been completely throttled, that idea of education with which we began. We've both been in that business for a very long time and it's gone from us. I would say that that the economic growth you mentioned in your questioning, and in your discussion with me, as something you were really looking forward to. That, and that 'Poverty would disappear'. I think that's something we should focus on a little bit in terms of who has an idea of India.

THAPAR. Let's also clarify that one isn't throwing the baby out with the bathwater—it's not that one is against the idea of economic growth at all, especially economic growth related to poverty. That is absolutely fundamental. All that's happened, of course, is that we continue with our failures on that score, except that now the talk is about development. The new mantra is development—everybody makes a speech, and says, 'We're for development'. What is meant by this? We're never told in detail, but we're for it. What I was trying to emphasize was not that the obsession with economic growth was the fault. But that one had to also give some importance to other factors, and that we failed to do so. And one among those was the question of caste.

I remember, in the 60s and 70s, there was little discussion on social inclusion. One *was* well intentioned and thought, 'Caste had to be got rid of,' but little was done in a fundamental way to make it the kind of thing that you can slowly slide out of your system. On the contrary: it's around that time that the use of caste identities in politics starts to be recognized. Nehru's original idea of universal franchise was that every individual has a vote, and that is what would make the person independent. Because he will vote the way he wishes to vote, and parties will have to woo the voter on that basis. But the reverse has happened—there are now vote banks, and elections are based on vote banks, and the parties are not wooing the independent vote but only the right vote bank. And I think this is really a negation of democracy. Another negation is the increasing dependence on defections. A party gets the majority not by being elected in the required numbers but by making up the number through getting elected persons to defect from one party to another. In a way this makes fun of the electorate, but then who cares. It's a very worrying situation, but isn't seen that way. No one is facing the issue in terms of: How are you going to convert a hierarchical society into a less hierarchical society? You can't remove the hierarchy altogether, but can you make it less so?

And this is where, actually, I think there are two aspects that are fundamental. Again, slightly touched on in the 60s but not very much. One was, as you said, education. We, at that stage, still had an education system that did up to a point teach people how to think. That's gone completely. Encouraging students to ask questions is frowned upon. And we have politicians who must *not* say, 'You ask questions.' Whereas for some of us, the basis of education is that you teach students how to ask questions. That hasn't happened. Partly I think because it was also tied up in the issue of which language was the medium of instruction. I may, again, be completely wrong but I think that, possibly, if we'd had a dual-language system—the local, regional language and English—that there might have been much more questioning. I say this simply because the kinds of books that one reads, critical books, in English, tend to question much more than the books published in the local languages. Now this is not true of every language. There are some which are more advanced, perhaps because they have better translations, perhaps they have people that are more analytical who are writing. But I think that input from a different kind of intellectual tradition is always a very worthwhile input. Otherwise, one does get very bogged down in just one intellectual tradition.

And if you really go into the question of language, the intellectual tradition as expressed, for example, in Hindi and as expressed in Malayalam is not the same. There is a difference. I'm not going to comment on which I think is better because that's not the issue, but there is a difference. And I think that one has to recognize that something coming in from elsewhere does force people to think beyond what they're taught in their own tradition.

Apart from language, the content of education is central, and here I'd like to bring in the discussion on secularism. During the time of the national movement, we did not endorse the Hindu Rashtra idea and say that the Hindu has primacy as a citizen. The second aspect, which is again where I think we didn't discuss the issue of secularism sufficiently, is the question of not just the coexistence of religions but also of their equal status and even more importantly, the extent to which religious organizations control social institutions. And education is a very important factor there. The content of education depends on who is controlling the content and who is financing education, especially in a so-called secular state. Now of course we're running into problems because state education is far from being secular any more. As long as you had a reasonably secular state, it was possible to have the content of education not coloured by the strength and importance of local religious organizations. That's a very important factor in the question of secularism. So education is one area where I think we should've taken a much stronger stand when these issues came up in the 70s.

The first big debate on textbooks was in the time of the Morarji Desai government, after the Emergency, when those of us who had written the first lot of NCERT textbooks were being attacked by those that did not want secular history. I think the period after that was when we should have insisted much more forcefully on removing the textbooks from government control. We tried, but not hard enough. We realized that government control could be damaging, but eventually let it be.

The second aspect that needs much more discussion than what we give it at the moment is the question of civil law.

Do we in fact continue with civil law according to religious conventions? In a sense, a step was taken in that direction with the Hindu Code Bill in 1956, which was of course attacked viciously when it was first brought up and which we forget. But that was just an attempt to try and clean up one religious code relating to civil law. Now we have many—not only religious codes like the Muslim Personal Law and the Hindu Code Bill but also Khap Panchayats in Haryana which are caste laws, caste laws which result in killings if they are broken. The point is: Isn't it time that we removed all the individual laws of caste and religion, and reformulated a civil code that is truly secular?

These two things, the content of education and civil laws, are very important items in the creation of the idea of India, the identity of the Indian and the kind of society one looks forward to.

SPIVAK. Who are the *we*? Since I spend most of my time away from us secularists . . . and of course I'm completely for secular law, no problem there at all. I remember Amartya Sen once calling me from Rome, saying, 'I'm sorry I said you were someone who supports fundamentalism, because you work with subaltern studies.' I said, 'Amartya, at least you're calling me because you felt bad, because you know damn well I'm not.' I'm not a fundamentalist. But it is true that there is a possibility of finding the world-historical by bringing this public discourse of religion to a crisis, a discourse we can no longer, at all, support. If we do, we are not being secular. We have to behave as if religion is like going to the bathroom—completely private, shut the door. However, that's not reflected in the world. And so we may pass the law, but it will be like that line from Shakespeare, 'I can call the spirits from the vasty deep.' I have secular laws. 'Why, so can I, or so can any man; But will they come, when you do call for them?' That's what Hotspur responds. So from that point of view, I think one of the most difficult things is to de-transcendentalize—sorry for that word, but you know that I'm a very obscure person—the religious which can work even at the grassroots level. I hate the word grassroots, but you know what I mean—I say they're bottom-feeders. Even at that level it can work, because when it's not mobilized politically, then this happens. Like in Bangladesh: I'm eating kurbaan meat with very, very poor people. They don't eat meat because they are too poor. Yet I'm eating meat, so they say, 'Didi. Amra khacchi toh thik ache, apni keno khacchen?' We're eating, it's all right, but why are you eating beef, eh? They're protecting my religion. That is a certain kind of thing which can operate when it's not mobilized as a difference recognizing violence.

I remember the 200th anniversary of Presidency, Hindu College. I read the First Bishop of Calcutta in Middleton (it's published): These natives are so stupid that they think there are many

ways of approaching the Almighty,
whereas we know the right way. As in,
we cannot teach them the scriptures,
and therefore, they should go to
Murray's English Grammar, and I
approve of Hindu College.

Now why was this mistaken as
access to secular education? Why can't
we not think that a certain kind of class
mobility actually puts the lid on
religious cultures? There is so much of
it. This is again a story, like your story
about lowering the Union Jack.

Now I've been living with these
people for a very long time, 30 years
now. So they have finally come to
accept that I behave in this way, maybe
because I live in the United States. Fine.
But one day I take a slice of tomato
from the side of someone's plate and I

eat it, without thinking. And there is this huge silence for about 75 seconds. These are the people I work with, live with, eat with, everything, but a Brahman has eaten from his jhootha plate! You see, they believe this damn thing! In order to undo this, we can't just put secular laws in place—nobody will internalize them.

So I feel that we really ought to think of who the 'we' are. Development is insertion into the circuit of capital without any kind of training as to how to manage it. Forget the training to use capital for social ends. All these swanirbhar schemes with their bank accounts, etc.—yet nothing is taught about how to manage them. Hence development and the question of language within development.

I teach English in the United States. And I will say that one can't have confidence in English texts being more impartial. Mind you, at the same time, I will agree with you that it doesn't mean local-language texts should be celebrated. But I must say that my confidence in English-language texts has really gone somewhere after these 30 years of hanging out with these other people. And I will also say this, that the idea of the Global South, a deeply reverse-racist idea which totally ignores class, is now up for sale. Because they do this English thing in a very superficial way, with no knowledge at all. They are proposing these alternative epistemologies, and that too is a deeply troublesome thing.

So the entire question of what to do with languages. Again, I will go off the topic: one of my projects, which will never be funded because it's Central Africa, is about the unwritten languages, the wealth of unwritten languages, survivor/survival languages, campaigners campaigning in them so that there is ethnic violence right before the elections, etc. Languages which the UN in its wisdom thinks need 'preservation'—'They're going extinct and they should be preserved.' To an extent this is a question that goes beyond India, it's a global question.

I'm sorry I spoke at such length. But with regard to both the question of secularism and the question of English scholarship, English-language and European-language scholarships—one

has to think about the concept of
sanctioned ignorance. And about the
idea of what to do with languages that
are in an unexamined way being called
better than English. This is a fraught
field.

THAPAR. Yes it is a very fraught field, and
one's fully aware of that. But the point
of course is that you're here. I'm not
going into the international dimensions,
the global dimensions, because that's
huge, and you're quite right that it's a
problem which seems to be beyond
solving. But with us: Are we moving
towards a future where precisely these
languages, the hundreds of languages
that, maybe don't have a script, or have
a script, are spoken—what is going to
happen to them? Are the Munda-
speaking people having to convert

completely to Hindi in order to survive, or can they be bilingual, and reach out to people far beyond just their one language area? This is also a problem in demography, because what you've got today is a degree of migration in this country that you've never had before. Landless labour going all over the place, from Kerala to Punjab, from Punjab to Assam—crossing huge distances. What is going to happen to the languages when people grow up in an area where their own family speaks one language but everybody else speaks another, and they can't go out because they don't know the third language and the third language is important. Are we going to have people being inward-looking all the time? Are cultures going to become like ingrown toenails?

SPIVAK. No.

THAPAR. No?

SPIVAK. No. It's a very gendered question of
course. The third-language thing also
really affects gendering because access
to language is highly gendered. Now the
students here, the people who go to
Kerala and so on to break stones, or put
coffee in bags, many of them are my
students, you know, because there's no
jobs here. They're not happy . . .

Anyway, what happens is not
something we can control. It's a kind of
general realization, and takes a little
time. Because these ideas, they're old
twentieth-century, nineteenth-century
linguistic ideas, of languages in boxes,
names, orthography, etc. Since 1986,
I've been hanging out with these so-
called Aboriginals and they are in fact

bilingual. They were speaking Magadh, Prakit—not the Kheriya language as many people in the cities thought. They were also speaking in Bengali to me, constantly, and saying, 'Didi, learn our language.' The Mundas and Oraons in Birbhum, for example. Now they're also doing a little Oraon stuff on the side, which is wonderful. But what happens is that this dialectal continuity, this multilinguality on the surface, we don't even know about this. It's not like there is a general creolization. It's more like the ecology of forests. So this whole huge thing about, 'Oho, language extinct, let's preserve'—that's not what's happening in real life. What's happening at the top of linguistics now is an acknowledgement that those unwritten languages are completely dialectally continuous, very multilingual, etc.

Those are not like the big lingua francas, you know, esiZulu, and kiSwahili, and so on. They are the survivor/survival languages—pre-scientifically digitized, written on the memory. So they're not tied down to that old idea of named languages in boxes. These linguists are really at work on this. It will not be like the other languages, about which we ask: What to do with it? For the purpose of globality, we should keep English and French and Russian and Chinese and so on.

THAPAR. No, I don't think for a moment that it's going to be like the twentieth century—it's bound to be different. But it's precisely that difference that we have to be aware of. What is the difference—and the difference is not just language. Bilingualism alone will not solve it, nor the cross-lingual use of languages. It's tied into one's professional work, marriage relations, how far one migrates, and all the rest of it. It's a very complex question. What I'm trying to argue is that, instead of looking at just the one strand, whether it be economic growth, whether it be caste, whether it be religion, one has to look at the totalities, and the intermeshing of these totalities which we have ceased to do now. In the 60s, though I felt there was an obsession with economic growth, there was some concern, not enough but some concern, with the other aspects. People were very worried about the fact that religion was beginning to enter education, law and professional activity. Religiosity was on the increase. But there were no solutions to that, or people didn't think about them sharply enough, strongly enough. Now, of course, you don't think about them at all—you just let it all ride as it's riding. And one is looking at the future and saying, 'But do people realize what this riding is going to lead to?' And the kind of interlinkages that one had always hoped would be fundamental to the kind of society one's going to build, those interlinkages don't exist any more. People don't think along those lines.

SPIVAK. In *The Fourth Industrial Revolution* written by the director of the World Economic Forum, Klaus Schwab, there's this sentence, 'It depends on us.' And I think that's what's changed. I don't think it's really up to us to build the society but to acknowledge how interlinkages are happening, the interlinkages we cannot quite imagine through the training we have had. So learning to learn the things that don't resemble the kinds of plans, if you don't mind my quoting Marx—that sentence I always quote—'The content of the nineteenth-century revolutions will come from the poetry of the future.' That's Karl Marx: 'poetry of the future'. Interlinkages will happen, not all good, some really, really scary, but we will not be able to plan them because we are building a society.

THAPAR. The interlinkages are there. My point is that we are not giving enough attention to the fact that they're there. That we're not looking at them—we're picking up only one thread, and then just going on and on about that one thread. Whether it's religion or caste or economy, it doesn't matter. The connections are not being made, that's all.

SPIVAK. Talking about curricular change. I'm just coming from Durban, where a brother was talking wonderfully about how you have to have terminology to teach algebra in esiZulu. No, no, no, I said: 'Look, I went to a good school but it was Bengali-medium up to Class 7. So when we learnt algebra, etc., we were learning in Bengali. We used words like equation, formula, etc., while learning in Bengali, but those nouns were there. And now, when I coach the high-school students—I didn't even know that algebra was *beejgonit*. I know now. I don't know the Bengali word for formula, and I don't know the Bengali word for equation. On the other hand, if my authority is undermined, then the kids will lose confidence. So I'm saying to my supervisor, 'Ei, pata ulto, pata ulto, turn the pages, see where it's used for the first time, prothom bar byabohaar hoyeche, bojha jabe Bangla ta ki. What is the Bengali of formula, and what is the Bengali of equation.'

This way of lexicalizing the superior into the general linguistic medium which is totally creolized—it's extremely difficult for people like you and me to imagine this, because we don't do it. It totally doesn't resemble what we do. Especially if you're teaching languages, right? I could give more examples but I think I'm becoming a bit absurd. But this is what

I would say: that the general creolity of the world, on a certain level, without our progressive bourgeois ideas of building societies, and so on and so forth, is taking something away . . .

Just one more story. I used to go to those mud schools near the Laos border where they'd never seen non-Chinese foreigners. So those schools—one person, one community, one school—they've been closed down. Now with some private money, the state has opened central schools, they're like prisons. They wrote a thing in Chinese for me, talking about the fact that in those one-community, one teacher-schools, which are very remote, in the Himalayas near Laos, they were teaching what they call ethics, which is socialism. Nobody talks to these people—there are no non-Chinese foreigners there at all. But the guy is showing me the rubber stuff coming in, right? 'Look,' he says, 'five years ago when I showed you all the trucks bringing rubber, it was the same amount of rubber. Today you will see, some are more, some are less. We have lost our one-room mud schools.' See, there's stuff going on. They won't win in the way we recognize winning, but one hopes that this level of stuff will become the poetry of the future. I'm sorry if I talk like a literary person, what can you do, that's what I am.

THAPAR. I think that's about all one can ask for. You can't ask for the idea of society, but a little move in that direction would be very encouraging. And it's that little move that one doesn't see in what's going on. It's simply not happening, and however much one may converse, and however much one may go out and talk to people, somehow it is not being understood. And that in a sense is what I find most depressing, that now we are in a situation where we can make the kinds of changes we had thought of making in the 60s. But we are stymied by the fact that we're not recognizing what is happening.

SPIVAK. We are not acknowledging that we may have to shift class focus in order to be able to. You're older than I am, but I feel very much that I'm too old, you know . . .

THAPAR. My god, I'm not feeling that for a long time.

SPIVAK. You're so full of energy, Romila—

THAPAR. No no. You know, I wish to goodness the next generation would take over more efficiently.

SPIVAK. In this way, we can perhaps see a mahan Bharat, eh? Then it would be something different, won't it? Yeah. What does that mean?

THAPAR. Should we stop on that note?

SPIVAK. I think so. And you know what they say on Air India these days? They're obliged to, after every announcement. 'Jai Hind'.